Try Your Hand

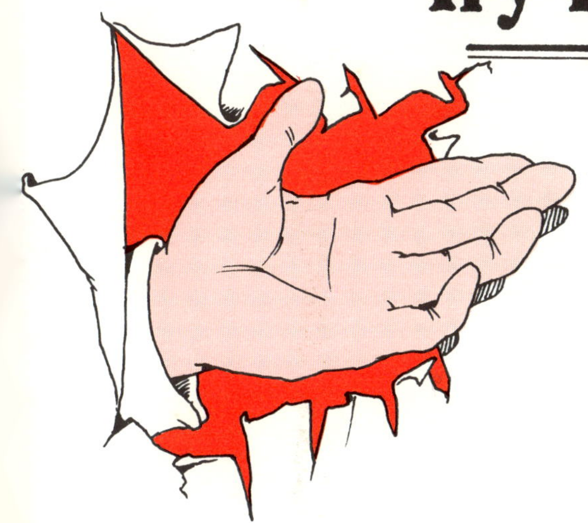

by Jane Thayer

illustrated by Joel Schick

William Morrow and Company
New York 1979

This book is dedicated to Maud
with my gratitude and my affection.

Text copyright © 1980 by Jane Thayer
Illustrations copyright © 1980 by Pongid Productions

Library of Congress Cataloging in Publication Data

Woolley, Catherine.
  Try your hand.
  Summary: Uses riddles and phrases to show the wide variety of meanings of the word "hand."
  1. English language—Terms and phrases—Juvenile literature. 2. Hand (The English word)—Juvenile literature. 3. Riddles—Juvenile literature. [1. Hand (The English word) 2. English language—Terms and phrases] I. Schick, Joel. II. Title.
PE1689.W6   428'.1 [E]   79-18608
ISBN 0-688-22215-3   ISBN 0-688-32215-8 lib. bdg.

Printed in the United States of America
1 2 3 4 5 6 7 8 9 10

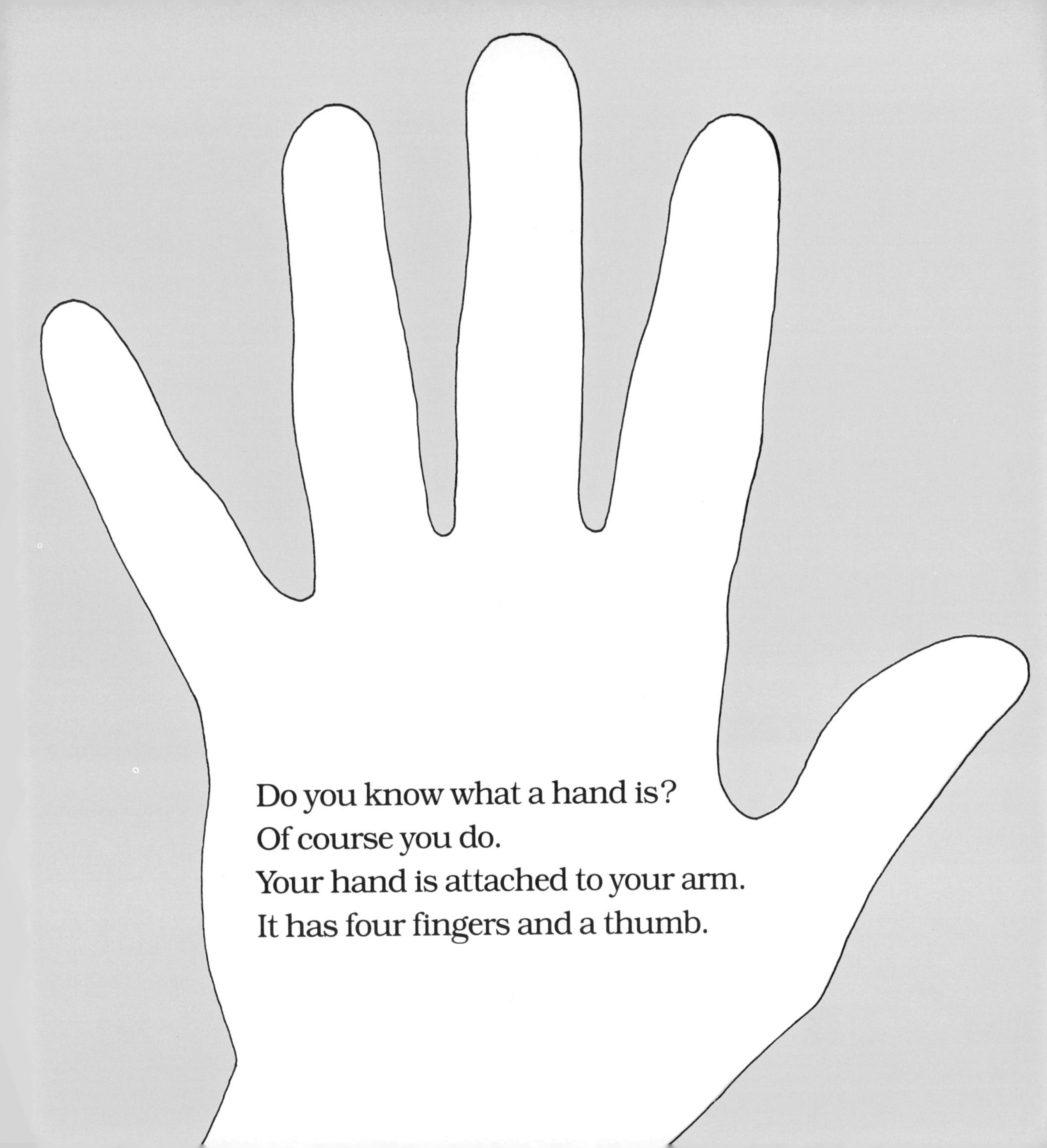

Do you know what a hand is?
Of course you do.
Your hand is attached to your arm.
It has four fingers and a thumb.

You do things with it
like eat, wave, dig, get dressed,
brush teeth . . .

... turn the page.

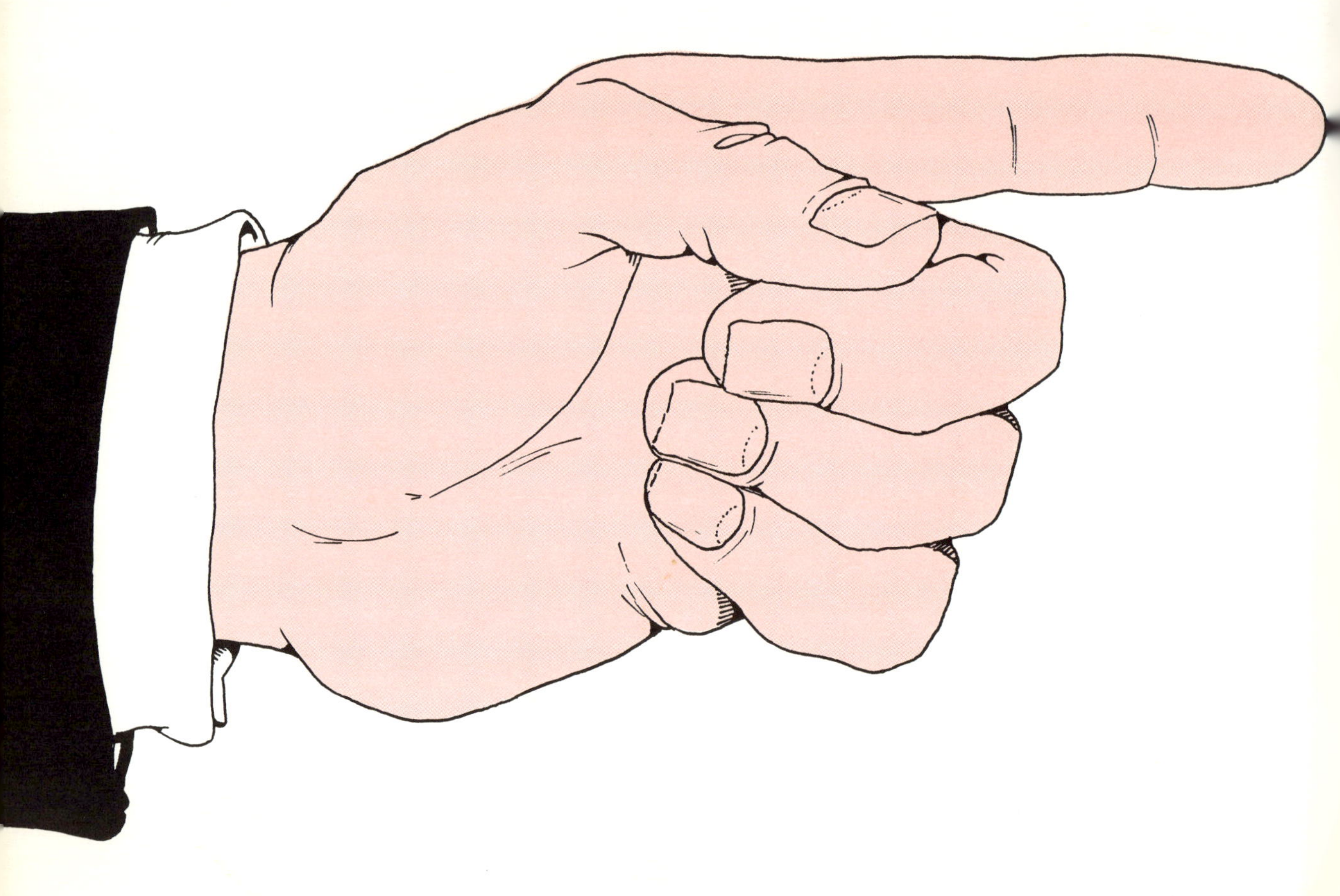

But there are other kinds of hands.
For instance,
some hands are always marking time.
What kind of hands are they?

11 12 1
10 2
9 3
8 4
7 6 5
TIME ON
MY HANDS....
MADAME MANO
PALMIST
HOURS BY APPOINTMENT

The **hands** of a clock.

What kind of hand
do you love to hold? 

A winning **hand**!

What kind of hand
yellows with age
but never shows a wrinkle? 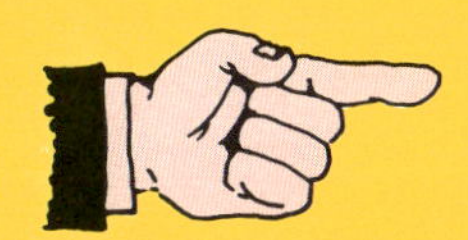

HEY--WILL SOMEBODY
GIVE ME A HAND WITH
THESE BANANAS?

A **hand** of bananas.
The name for
a large cluster of them.

What kind of hand
can't always expect
smooth sailing? 

MORGAN

A deck**hand**.
"All hands on board!"
said the captain.

What kind of hand
do you give
the winning team? 

MUSH
CLAP
CLAP
CLAP
CLAP
CLAP
CLAP
FINISH LINE

A big **hand**.

What hand has been at it
for years? 

I'M AN OLD COWHAND
FROM THE RIO GRANDE--

An old **hand**.

What kind of hand
is a pitcher?

BALE FOUR!

A farm**hand**.
He pitches hay.

When do you use a hand
instead of a foot? 

AND BE SURE
YOUR HANDS
ARE WARM!
6

When you measure a horse.
A horse is not so many *feet* high.
It is so many **hands** high.
Each one of these hands
measures four inches.

What kind of hands
does a good guy have? 

HANDS UP, SHERIFF!
NICE 'N' CLEAN, AIN'T THEY?

Clean **hands**.

What can money do
that you can't do? 

NOW, THERE MUST BE A NICKEL IN HERE SOMEWHERE!

Change **hands**.

What kind of hand
can you lend?

CAUTION:
QUICKSAND

A helping **hand**.

What kind of hand
is a neat trick? 

THE HAND IS QUICKER THAN THE EYE-- OOPS!
BUT NOT AS QUICK AS THE RABBIT!
RANDY

Sleight-of-hand.

You finally did that job
so what did you get? 

FIDO
WET
PAINT

You got it off your **hands**!

What's the least you can do
to solve these riddles? 

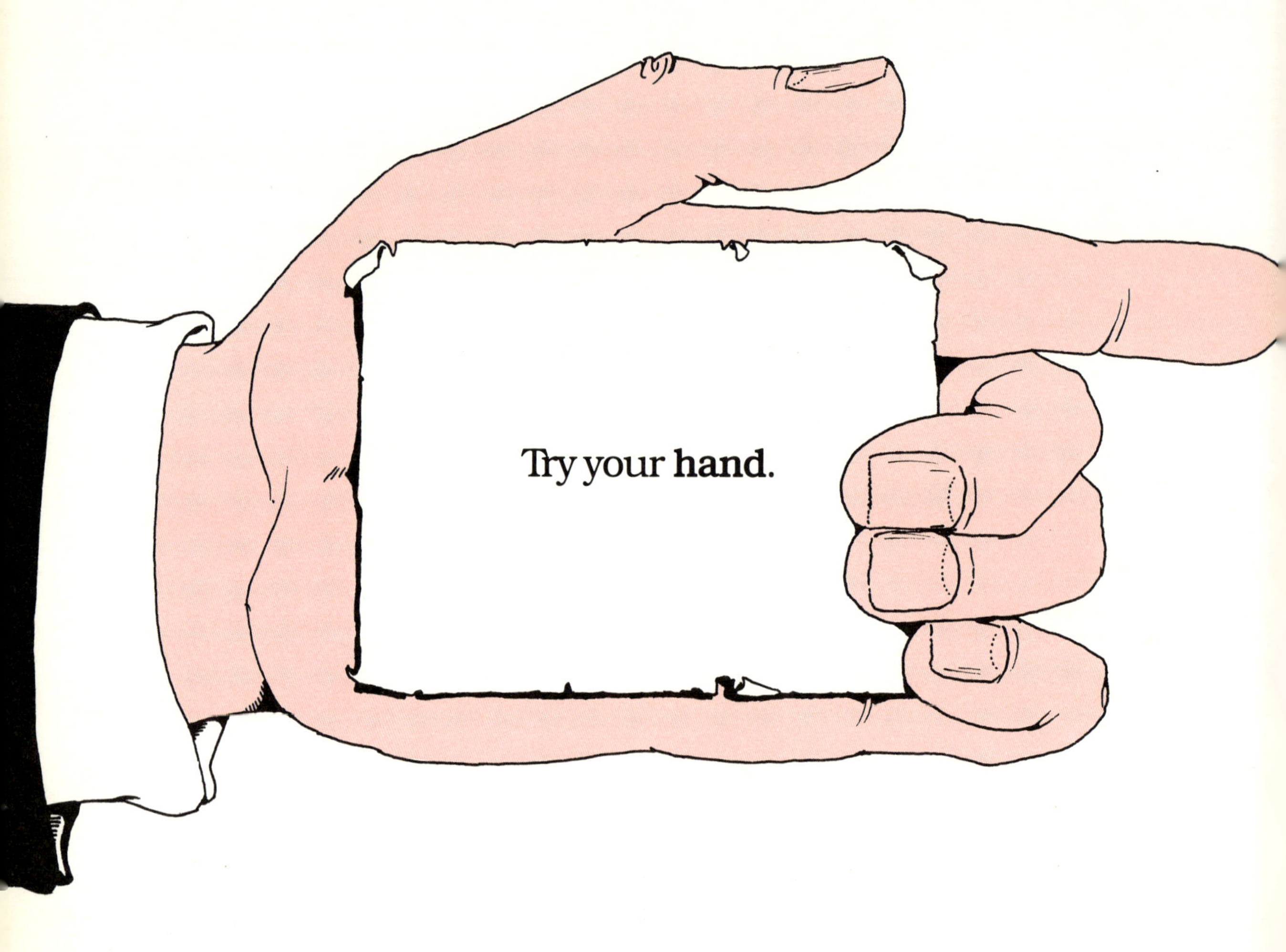

Try your hand.

THEN THERE'S…
on hand   off hand
at hand
out of hand
on this hand   on that hand
on every hand
on one hand
on the other hand
first hand
second hand
right-hand man
glad hand
handmade
hand-me-down
handout
Don't bite the hand that feeds you.
Did you have a hand in that?
Your left hand doesn't know
    what your right hand's doing.
stagehand
free hand
safe hands
in good hands

Do you know what a hand is?
Good question!

About the Author

Jane Thayer is the pen name Catherine Woolley uses for her picture books. Her first William Morrow picture book, *The Horse with the Easter Bonnet,* was published in 1953. She has written many others since, including the popular series that features the ghost named Gus.

The author was born in Chicago but spent many years in Passaic, New Jersey, where she was involved in numerous community activities. She now lives in an old house on Cape Cod.

About the Illustrator

Joel Schick was born in Chicago, Illinois, and earned a B.A. there at Roosevelt University. In 1968, he began working as a book designer and art director, and then, in 1975, he became a full-time illustrator. His wife, Alice, is a writer of children's books, and they live with their son in Monterey, Massachusetts.